I0706688

Is It Over?

Elle Rain

This collection is dedicated to anyone who has felt or
feels like their heart cannot heal.
Thank you to everyone who has read my work in the
drafting stages, helped with edits and supported me
through this journey (you know who you are)

I have been wanting to write this collection for almost
ten years, so I am very nervous and excited to share
this with you.

Copyright @ 2024 written and illustrated by Elle Rain
Published by Kindle Direct Publishing

The honeymoon phase

I remember slow dancing with our souls
in the middle of downtown
every eye was on us
but the only one I was watching was you

Your kisses were soft
long and slow
each with such intention
I could feel them in my toes

Your eyes showed me a galaxy
no telescope could compete
the constellations danced and
twinkled every time you looked at me

looking at the stars no longer does me justice

I've never felt more comfortable
in a stranger's arms
than our first embrace

One single whisper of the wind
sends goosebumps down my neck
as if it were your breath

You have no idea what you continue to do to me
even after all these years

I crave the curve of your lips
pressed against mine
the taste of your strawberry chapstick
as you bite my lip

After meeting you
no one will ever have all of me again

My finger drawing over the canvas of your body
tracing every line and muscle indentation
creating an invisible masterpiece of
pleasure

You're my muse for everything I write
down to the little doodles on the edge of my pages

When you liked someone in kindergarten there was no fear of rejection. You may have handed your crush a heart you cut out of red construction paper and they either kept it or tore it up, but it never got you down. If you liked someone you may have teased them or pushed them on the swing, but no matter how you showed it, you were never afraid to. When does this fear start?

Laying in bed with you
our intertwining hair creating an array of colors
commingling creating the most beautiful
dark auburn brown hair

The mold of your body lying next to mine
forever
imprinted on this mattress

Your body
my comfort

your words
my inspiration

you'll forever be my muse

Let's dance in the diner where we had our first date
you kissed me so soft
I got swept away

You've seeped into every inch of my body
making my skin buzz
with the slightest touch

I want to put on fancy outfits, even though part of us
would both rather stay in. Pretend we know how to
dance and go out on the town, and you'll twirl me until
we both fall down.

Lead me to your bedroom and show me the pretty
shapes we can make in the sheets
when we're done
let's admire the art we've created

A million words shuffle through my mind
every message I send
wanting to confess my love to you
but all I say instead is
hey you

Your words are on every song I have ever listened to
your tongue touches the food that goes into my mouth
the wind leaves traces of your scent
just when you've been out of my mind too many days
I can taste you and smell you and hear you
everywhere I go

Our first touch was an explosion of emotions
wanting to bottle the feeling
when our bodies first collided
to experience
over and over

Walking around the city lights, we found a dimly lit alleyway, music filled the streets from the boombox on the 3rd floor apartment. They were having a party, the party of the year, laughter, shrills and the most gatsby-esque feelings flooded the streets, but you and I had our eyes only on each other, and we danced the night away in the dimly lit alleyway.

I wish you knew what my heart was doing the first time
I saw you
how fast my heartbeat was during our first embrace
I was sure you were going feel it
through my winter coat

when I saw you through the see through glass door for
the first time
I wasn't even sure I'd be able to make to you
upright
the butterflies were swarming every inch of my body

I remember sitting by the pond
a warm summer night
getting eaten alive for hours
because we didn't want to say goodbye

I drove home at 5am with the sunrise and morning
birds chirping and I still felt your embrace even after I
walked away

Long distance

I can feel the pressure of your hand on my neck
pulling me in for the most passionate kiss
but my head falls back in response
to the emptiness of air
keeping my head afloat

Even from miles away
your words are my safety

You have an aura
full of color
exuding a rainbow with every spoken word
but with every selfless act
you shed a color in response

Do you still drink your coffee black?

I never knew the last time we embraced
would be our last

Things you've done to me that you have no idea:

made me realize I cannot truly love anyone else again

The sun was setting into a purple cotton candy swirl
as the waves crashed on the shore
the seagulls swarmed the left behind picnic food from
who knows when

this was supposed to be our real first date
we had planned it for months
but now I sit here alone
watching the seagulls tear each other apart
for stale food
with a picnic basket for one

The memories of you stay rent free in my mind
taking up the largest square footage available
       - when you think of someone everyday

I would jump on a plane any day
any time
for you

I remember staying up as late as I could just so I could say good morning and you'd set your alarm for ten minutes early just so you could say goodnight

You describe the way you kiss me over text
in a way I can feel your lips on mine
when I sleep at night and daydream at noon
missing your lips on mine
but your words will have to do

In an alternate universe
long distance may have worked
but all I'm left with are memories of 5 hour video calls
with the occasional snack and bathroom break
and a never-been-carved spot on my mattress

We're the stereotypical hallmark movie trope of "will-they won't-they" and that's fine in the rom coms because they always end up together and they're just actors, and even if they fell in love in real life they get paid to do this. But why am I settling for a will-they won't-they when at our best I'm getting less than fifty percent.

Funny how long distance relationships cause you to
get closer
faster
because of the chunks of time spent together

but when you are together
as much as the flame burns quickly
the wick turns to ash at the same rate

~~You would have blown up my life~~
You blew up my life.

you allowed me to think about things I would never
dare to dream
you taught me to love myself by loving me
I would have uprooted my life
for a chance at a new one with you

They all told us long distance never works
I just wanted to prove them wrong

Hi, I see you live 5,000 miles away from me, but I
keep seeing your face in my dreams, and I needed to
reach out and just see by chance if you also think
about me
    -    things I wish I could say

When your story ended before it even began
-      long distance relationships

The problem with being in a long distance relationship

when the most exciting thing happens
and I just have to tell you about it
I have to wait over 10 hours to see your pixelated face
on my screen

My heart skips a little beat every time I see your name
pop up on my phone screen

They say butterflies happen in the honeymoon phase
but it's a been a year
and the butterflies have cocooned
and been reborn more times than I can count
they're hyperactive with every stolen glance
message sent
every time you say my name
they've made a permanent home inside my heart

I've memorized every angle of your face so I can picture you perfectly in my dreams

In a room with everyone I know and love
I'd go directly to you

I'd find you in any life

My heart shattered in pieces you couldn't see
one message completely altered the course of my life
realizing I was the only one
who could pick these pieces up
unlike the times before
I left them drowning in my college bedroom

Do you miss our favorite coffee house?
the smell of the roasting beans
hot paninis
and burnt toast
memories rush back
attacking every chance I have of moving on

Do you ever think about what waking up next to me would have been like?

The nape of your neck fit so beautifully in my hand
I can almost feel your breath on my lips as I
grasp for the air

Your pet names for me roll off my tongue
as I lay awake
wondering who you're using them for now

Lamenting on the ghosts of my past
you're awake
inside me

My eyes glaze over reading the tension build up to
their first kiss in the romance novel that could have
been our story

How can I get comfortable knowing the only person
who ever gave me that warmth
is covering someone else now

Our bedroom was going to be green
we had decided this early on
I lay awake with the white walls never have been
touched with color

Sometimes you can wait too long to say I love you

Does my scent ever cross your path
when you walk the dog that would have been ours
a slight aroma in the air
of jasmine and rose
the perfume you loved so much
that makes you think of me?

I've written you too many love letters
I will never send

I still picture us in our older years
sitting around your grandpa's handmade wooden table
in the one bedroom house they called home
drinking shitty wine and reminiscing on our lives
in my mind
this image is alive

Dreams are a powerful thing
but I realized my life shifted
when I started to look more forward to going to sleep
just in case you wander in my mind each night

We realized our love too late
so we go to sleep
hoping our dreams
keep the giddy teenage love alive

The motion of our hips
created a music
I'll never hear again

Our language we created
slowly forgotten
as you build your new life with
her
rewriting a conversation
you forgot you once already had

I watch the flame of my favorite candle
slowly deteriorate
into ash

We could never agree on how to hold hands
we both wanted under
        -      maybe a red flag

My notebook has seen your surname
written with mine
in every signature possible
but now those pages lay crumpled up in a bin
        -    your name will always sound better

Do I still love you? Or do I just love the memories

Watching an 80s rom com
believing maybe for a minute this could be our story
star crossed lovers finally finding their way back
to each other
but when the commercial comes on
I remember it's just a movie

and you've already moved on

What happens when you don't end up with your soulmate?

I'll never get to taste your lips again

Every summer
making freshly squeezed lemonade
filling the house with a beautifully sweet and sour
aroma
it was your favorite scent

I haven't had lemonade since

I keep you in my dreams because
I've created a love story for us so
intense
perfectly laid out in every way possible
and I know in my dreams I can replay these memories
over and over

but when I wake up
it's just a dream
and my heart aches for the next sleep

When I think about you
I think about what could have been
but that isn't real
and in my mind we live in a beautiful home
with our animals
playing music every day
but it isn't real
and it never happened

Hey you
even after all these years
you're the most attractive human I've ever met
all of the cliches about smiles and faces
you can't forget
you exude all of them
your personality
intoxicating
engulfing everyone who crosses your path
your hair falls down in waves like a waterfall
you just cannot leave
hey you
I still love you

    -    love letters I'll never send

Did you ever love me?

Our license for love expired the moment you
questioned if we would make it
giving me loads of paperwork with no opportunity for
renewal

I ~~can~~ will never rewrite our memories

I knew the first time we talked I would be in trouble
I could see it in your eyes
you were never going to fall for me
the way I fell for you
          -    confessions

Why didn't you let me love you?

I don't know if could ever be happy
not knowing what your lips felt on mine

Every day
arguably
we're slowly dying

but nothing feels like death more than knowing you're
thousands of miles away and our scents never got to
embrace

The dangerous world of daydreaming
is asking yourself what if and why
too many times
creating worlds that may never come true in your mind

And I have to settle for being friends
because the thought of you not being in my life
in some way
feels like a thousand open cuts
on the inside of my body

When will you stop making guest appearances in my dreams?

We had really big dreams, traveling the world in a van
living off the grid
with all our found animals
but most importantly the fear of not being together
never once crossed our minds.
           -     how quickly a month can change

Maybe we weren't supposed to make it
maybe our time was supposed to be cut short
maybe you were supposed to stay there
and I was supposed to stay here

Our love was like a broken oar
but only I was rowing a boat for two and
when it came down to saving us both
the broken oar chose you
leaving me to pick up the pieces
of my shipwrecked heart
while you didn't even look back to see
who was behind you

Healing?

I had another dream about you last night, but this time
it wasn't me you ended up with. She was tall and
brunette, with a super sweet smile, who held you with
everything she had and was everything you needed to
be happy.

I found out at my birthday dinner with my family
and I was

Okay

Maybe I wasn't pretty enough
skinny enough
funny enough

maybe I wasn't lady like enough
swore too much
cried too much

maybe I wasn't what you wanted
but I am exactly who I should be

-    Things I have to keep telling myself

The dreams returned briefly and for a minute
I was lost in your blue gray green eyes
looking into the milky way of colors
I cried
I awoke to my under eyes tight and cold
I missed you

It is so much easier to fantasize about someone else's life and wish you were in their shoes. But their shoes are different sizes and no matter how you wear them, you'll never walk comfortably.

Healing isn't linear (or at least that's what they say) but what happens when it's cyclical and you fall into the same movements every day just to keep your body from breaking down and when you can't take it any longer, your check engine lights on there's no mechanic that can fix it.

We had a beautiful memory garden
every seed planted a new
adventure lived
a memory garden with blooming
laughters
smiles
hugs and kisses
we cultivated this garden to have every flower we
wanted
but as time passed
our garden
wilted

I'm in love with someone who isn't real
I created a version of you that exists
and parts may be true
but we've been apart for so long
I can't remember your taste
and my brain is filling in the blanks where it wants

I remember the first morning I heard the birds sing
the first thought on my mind
their beautiful melodies
not
if I have woken to a message from you

The ache in my heart is slightly less today
our messages
a ghost town
abandoned after the storm raged through

digging through the pieces and debris
I've realized
you've forgotten all about me and that should hit me
like a dagger
but the ache in my heart is slightly less today

I didn't think about you today.

your lease expired without a warning and
the unlimited space in my mind I let you have
for *free*
cleared
I evicted the hold you had on me and
the regained space refilled with hobbies and laughter
and friends and
I didn't think about you today
for the first time in 2,290 days

I may never forget the curve of your lips
the way your nose slopes up in the perfect shape
and how your hair kisses your eyebrows

the color of your eyes the same as the ocean on a
cloudy morning with a hint of sun peaking through
but at the same time designed with constellations
dancing around

but I can't remember everything

I can't recognize your laugh anymore
the scent of you has become a blur
I get glimpses of it sometimes
but worn down and unfamiliar
your once gentle embrace I used to crave until my
heart hurt

I don't remember everything anymore

I've seen too many full moons since
the last time we talked
conversations that once took over my life
the eagerness to reply right away

the memories blurring between other random ideas
and to do lists
when you texted me
I forgot to even reply

One day I realized I didn't get a twinge in my heart
when I thought of you

I was out to a picnic with all of these wonderful
humans, eating delicious food and laughing and
playing silly card games and I didn't even realize it
but

I drank the lemonade.

If you've read this far, thank you so much, from the bottom of my heart. I have been really hesitant releasing this collection, but if it can help just one person heal or feel that they are not alone, then I'll feel like I did my job. If you don't have any other takeaways from this, let it be this: you're not alone, and you're worth fighting for. If you want to read more, or just say hi, find me on insta! Or email me at ellerainwrites@gmail.com